the treasury of

Clean

Teenagers'
Jokes

Look for the other books in
The Treasury of Clean Jokes series:

THE TREASURY OF

Clean
Teenagers'
Jokes

TAL D. BONHAM

BROADMAN
&HOLMAN
PUBLISHERS

Nashville, Tennessee

© 1997 by Tal D. Bonham

Printed in the United States of America

4263-61
0-8054-6361-5

Published by Broadman & Holman
Publishers, Nashville, Tennessee
Acquisitions and Development Editor:
Janis Whipple
Page Design:
Desktop Miracles, Inc., Addison, Texas

Dewey Decimal Classification: 808.87
Subject Heading: JOKES
Library of Congress Card Catalog Number:
96-53376

**Library of Congress
Cataloging-in-Publication Data**

Bonham, Tal D., 1934–91.
    The treasury of clean teenagers' jokes /
Tal D. Bonham. — 2nd. ed.

        p.   cm.
    Rev. ed. of: The treasury of clean teenage
jokes. © 1985.
    ISBN 0-8054-6361-5 (pbk.)
    1. Adolescent—Humor.   I. Bonham,
Tal D., 1934–91. The treasury of clean
teenage jokes.   II. Title.
PN6231.A26B66   1997
818'.5402—dc21

                            96-53376
                            CIP

97 98 99 00 01   2 3 4 5

Dedication

In 1991, Tal Bonham passed away,
leaving a legacy of both love and humor
to his family and friends,
and a legacy of laughter to all his readers.
In revising
The Treasury of Clean Teenagers' Jokes,
the publisher asked his wife
for a new dedication written
in memory of Tal D. Bonham.

In the past five years, since my husband's
heavenly homecoming,
his humor has enabled me,
my family, and those who loved him,
to cope with his loss.
Our four children agreed, at the time of selecting
the Scripture inscription on his tombstone,
that the following would be appropriate—

"A merry heart doeth good like a medicine"
(Prov. 17:22).

—Faye Bonham

Dedication

To the wonderful teenagers of
Dublin Baptist Church, Dublin, Ohio

Contents

Acknowledgments

Special thanks go to my wonderful wife, Faye, for her encouragement and help in the production of this book. She always has the final word—even in my writing!

A special word of appreciation is due Robert Larrimore for his support, his help in gathering material, and his many words of advice concerning this book.

It simply could not have been accomplished without the help of Mr. and Mrs. Charles Tommey. Thank you, Chuck and Dottie, for helping to put it together. From time to time, I know that your children—Charles, Janet, Cindy, and Sherri—also had a part in the project. Thanks, kids!

Thanks to Danny and Tal David—my two teenagers at home who gave me advice and encouraged me to "put one together for teens."

You helped, too, Randy—my college son whose friends at Cumberland College gave me some good ideas.

Marilyn (daughter), Wade (son-in-law), and Heather (our only grandchild) backed me from a distance—Thanks, kids!

My Gift to You

A teenage boy reported, "I took one of your joke books to class and shared it with my teacher. Each day he reads two or three jokes to our class before beginning his lecture."

"I carried one of your joke books to a slumber party," excitedly exclaimed a teenage girl. "We stayed up almost all night taking turns reading the jokes."

A cardiologist-friend of mine sent word, "While on a long automobile trip recently, I pitched one of your joke books into the back seat and encouraged my kids to pass the time by reading it to each other. We all had a great time laughing."

Several teenagers have asked, "Why don't you write a joke book just for us?" Well, here it is!

Every attempt has been made to eliminate humor that is questionable, sexist, or racist. Who says that we have to laugh at the expense of someone else?

Hey, kids! I hope you enjoy it!

—TAL D. BONHAM

Introduction

While speaking in a church recently, I met a woman with a sparkling personality and an amazing sense of humor.

In her earlier years she had lived the life of a juvenile delinquent. More than twenty years ago she became a Christian and has since dedicated her life to encouraging teenagers in trouble. With the help of her church and the encouragement of her husband, she has ministered to hundreds of teenagers through the years.

She shared a letter with me from a teenage boy whom she had visited in a youth detention center. It was an unusual letter. There was about a page and a half filled with information about him, his family, and the usual stuff teenage boys would share with an adult.

Then the letter said, "Here are some jokes."

1. What's yellow, sings, and weighs a thousand pounds?

ANSWER: Two five hundred-pound canaries.

What did the big beach ball say to the child?

ANSWER: "I get a kick out of you."

3. What do you get when you cross a mink and a kangaroo?

ANSWER: A mink coat with pockets.

4. What kind of room has no windows, no doors, and no walls?

ANSWER: A mushroom.

5. Why doesn't a motorcycle stand up?

ANSWER: Because it is two tired.

6. In what way is a teacher different from a train?

ANSWER: A teacher says, "Take out the gum," and a train says, "choo-choo."

This fine Christian lady said, "I have always used humor to bridge the gap between me and teenagers. If I can laugh with them, I can help them."

I love teenagers. I love to hear them laugh. I hope you will enjoy this little book of clean jokes.

Allowance

To some kids a high school education is four years of loaf on Dad's dough.

Neil walked into the living room and spoke to his father. "Pop," he said enthusiastically, "I've got great news for you!"

The father smiled and asked, "What is it?"

"Remember you promised me a five dollar allowance if I passed in school?"

The father nodded.

"Well," said Neil, "I'm sparing you that expense this year."

Don't bite the hand that has your allowance in it.

Arguments

Going out to meet trouble always proves to be one of life's shortest walks.

Rev. Darrell asked Kathy why she hit Chad with a chair.

"Because I couldn't lift the piano," she answered.

DAVID: "Whisper those three little words that will make me walk on air."

TARA: "Catch a plane."

A man was being questioned by the judge after a fight.

"Can you describe your assailant?" the judge asked.

"I don't want to, Judge," the man answered. "That's what I was doing when he hit me."

There are two sides to every argument, unless you are personally involved, in which case there is only one.

A man and his wife started out in the car after a quarrel. She sat in the back seat and continued to berate him for his faults. In her excitement she pounded on the car door and it flew open.

Several blocks later one of their neighbors flagged the man down. "Your wife fell out of the car back there," he said.

The man looked over at the back seat.

"Thank goodness," he said. "I thought I had lost my hearing."

Bores

A bore: A friend who isn't interested in hearing how well you did on your last test.

At a dinner, a rabbi was seated next to a pompous woman. "One of my ancestors," boasted the lady, "signed the Declaration of Independence."

"Is that so?" asked the rabbi. "One of mine wrote the Ten Commandments!"

Half of being smart is knowing what you're dumb at.

A minister was noted for his poor preaching, yet he was persistent in his efforts. One Sunday he announced, "There will be a meeting of the Board after the service."

When he finished his sermon, a small crowd of church officials gathered in one corner of the church to the right of the pulpit. In the back seat there was a stranger—a traveling man—who was spending Sunday in town.

"Good morning, stranger; can I do anything for you?" asked the minister.

"No, sir, but you said you wanted the bored to remain for a meeting, and I guess I was bored about as much as anyone!"

MATT: "What book are you reading?"
LEIGH ANN: "It's called, *What Millions of Girls Want.*"
MATT: "Did they spell my name correctly?"

An arrogant young salesman breezed into the one-horse town in his snappy convertible, screeched to a halt in front of the general store, and called to its owner, "Hey, old-timer, how long's this burg been dead?"

The old man looked up slowly, shifted his tobacco, and answered, "Um, not too long; you're the first buzzard's been around."

Boys

"Steve," screamed his mother, "you've been fighting again, and this time you've lost all your teeth!"

"No I haven't, Mom," protested Steve. "I got 'em right here in my pocket."

A backwoods couple were visiting a college campus with the thought of sending their daughter there. In the course of their sight-seeing, they came to the tennis courts where a girl and boy were playing.

"This is fine," said the father. "They keep them separated with a net up here."

Two boys were playing marbles together when a very pretty little girl walked by.

One boy stopped and said to his pal, "Boy, when I stop hating girls, she's the one I'm going to stop hating first!"

A Scoutmaster was determined that his Scouts should be ready for the next Court of Honor. He ordered each of them to be ready to report a good deed on the next night. When the boys had gathered, he began his questioning.

"What was your good deed for the day?" he asked.

"I helped an old lady across the street," the first Scout answered.

"Good." He turned to the next boy. "What was your good deed?"

"I helped him help the old lady across the street."

"I see." The Scoutmaster turned to the third boy. "What was your good deed?" he asked expectantly.

"I helped those two help the old lady across the street."

Frowning now, the Scoutmaster asked the fourth boy.

"I helped the other three guys help the old lady across the street."

"Now, look here," the Scoutmaster said sternly. "Why did it take four big boys to help one old woman across the street?"

"Because she didn't want to go."

Brothers

"What's Bob wailing about?" demanded a father of his older son.

Chris explained, "He's just crying because I'm eating my pie and won't give him any."

"Is his pie finished?" asked the father.

"It is," said Chris, "and he cried while I was eating that too."

Tom's mother was in the hospital, so he went to visit her and to see his new brother. Tom wandered into a room across the hall which was occupied by a woman with a broken leg.

"Hello," he said. "How long have you been here?"

"Oh, about a month."

"Can I see your baby?" he then asked.

"I don't have a baby," replied the woman.

"Gee, you're slow," said Tom. "My mama's been here just two days and she's got one!"

A father was consoling his angry son, advising he ought to meet his younger brother 50/50 on the matter. The boy replied, "What do you mean, I gave him 75 percent to start with!"

An older brother, going on five, watched his mother put a clean diaper on his baby brother. When she didn't dust the infant with talcum powder, the boy shouted, "Wait, Mother! You forgot to salt him."

"It's the little things in life that tell," said Dawn as she dragged her kid brother out from underneath the sofa.

Tony went to school one morning loaded down with a big bag of bubble gum which he passed out to his classmates. He even handed some to his surprised teacher, who asked, "What's this all about?"

"Oh," he answered, "I just became a brother last night."

The English teacher was irate. "This composition on "Our Cat,'" she exploded, "is word-for-word the same as your brother Dwight's."

"Yes, ma'am," came back Dwayne, "it's the same cat."

"Danny, why did you kick your little brother in the stomach?"

"He turned around."

A young boy was getting his third polio shot.

"Which arm would you like it in?" asked the doctor.

"Mother's!" replied the boy.

Two brothers wanted to ask a favor of their mother.

"You ask her," said the older brother.

"No," said the younger brother. "You ask her. You've known her longer than I have."

Camps

Young lady's diary
about her stay at summer camp:

First day—checked in; easy job; met Don who carried my suitcase;
Second day—Don asked me to go to the snack bar;
Third day—date with Don; he asked if he could kiss me; I refused;
Fourth day—I refused again and Don threatened that if I didn't kiss him, he would blow up the whole auditorium with three thousand people inside;
Fifth day—I saved three thousand lives tonight.

Camping Laws
1. The weight of your pack increases in direct proportion to the amount of food you consume from it.
2. The number of stones in your boot is directly proportional to the number of hours you have been on the trail.
3. The difficulty of finding any given trail marker is directly proportional to the importance of the consequences of failing to find it.

4. The remaining distance to your chosen campsite remains constant as twilight approaches.

5. The net weight of your boots is proportional to the cube of the number of hours you have been on the trail.

6. If you take your boots off, you'll never get them back on again.

7. The local density of mosquitos is inversely proportional to your remaining repellent.

"Camping out in the woods is fun," the family said *intently*.

The group of young men was sitting around a campfire. Their leader was lecturing on the hazards of camping out. "And boys," he warned, "you must be careful of snakes. If a snake bites someone on the leg, just take out your knife and crisscross the place where the snake bit him and suck out the poison. Are there any questions?"

"Sir," asked Spencer, "you say if a snake bites someone on the leg you cut it with a knife and suck out the poison? What do you do if a snake bites you on the posterior?"

"Well, son," replied the leader, "that's when you find out who your friends are."

"At camp, someone took my wallet and my trousers," the victim said *briefly*.

A boy, wearing his Boy Scout uniform, was asked by the scoutmaster, "What good deed did you do today?"

"Oh," said the boy, "Mother had only enough castor oil for one dose, so I let my sister take it."

"It appears this road doesn't lead out of the forest after all," the troop leader said *densely*.

A teenage boy on a camping trip with his friends wrote his mother a postcard: "Yesterday our leader took us on a mountain-climbing expedition. I wasn't too good, so I broke a leg. But don't worry—it wasn't one of mine."

Randy and Danny, whose younger brother had fallen into a pond, rushed home to Mother with tears in their eyes. "We're trying to give David artificial respiration," cried Danny, "but he keeps getting up and walking away."

Cars

Teenage Laws of Driving

1. You can get anywhere in ten minutes if you go fast enough.
2. Speed bumps are of negligible effect when the vehicle exceeds triple the desired restraining speed.
3. The vehicle in front of you is traveling slower than you are.
4. The lane you are in ends in five hundred feet.
5. At any level of traffic, any delay is intolerable.

A highway patrol officer asked a teenager why he was driving on the wrong side of the street. The teenager replied, "Why not, the other side is full!"

What is the best thing to take when you are rundown?

The number of the car that hit you.

Any tool dropped while repairing an automobile will roll under the car to the vehicle's exact geographic center.

"Hey, you can't park by the fire hydrant," yelled the policeman.

"Why not?" Lisa asked, "The sign says, 'Fine for Parking.'"

Little Heather was visiting her grandfather's farm for the first time. "Grandpa," she asked, "What kind of cow is that?"

"It's a Jersey cow."

"How can you tell? It's not wearing any license plates."

Jeep: a New York taxicab that's been drafted.

A safe journey on a busy expressway means you finished in the same car you started with.

> *Daddy bought a little car.*
> *And feeds it gasoline.*
> *And everywhere that Daddy goes*
> *He walks—his son's sixteen.*

A twelve-car pile-up means a driver's education student signaled for a left-hand turn and eleven people believed him.

A girl who just got her driver's license sat in a car wash for hours because she thought it was raining too hard to drive.

A teenager driving out of state for the first time saw a gas station sign a mile before the state line. The sign read: "Last chance for $1.50 gas."

So he filled up his car and, after paying, asked the attendant the price of gas in the next state. The attendant replied, "$1.20."

Appearing in traffic court is no fun, but the judge always has a fine time.

PHIL: "Dad, the Bible says if you don't let me have the car, you hate me."
DAD: "Where does it say that?"
PHIL: Proverbs 13:24. "He that spareth his rod hateth his son."

A Busy Expressway: a road that takes you fifty miles in twenty-five minutes flat . . . whether you want to go or not.

1. It's the only road in the world that you can travel on from one end to the other without once leaving the scene of the accident.
2. If you want to speed up your travel time, just move to the rear of the ambulance.

3. It ranks second to World War II as a cure for atheism.
4. One can always tell when one is approaching the expressway. One's St. Christopher statue gets down from the dashboard and climbs into the glove compartment.

The dilapidated old car wheezed up to the toll gate.

"Seventy cents," said the attendant.

"Sold," answered the teenage driver quickly.

Commotion

Laws of the Dorm

1. The amount of trash accumulated within the space occupied is exponentially proportional to the number of living bodies that enter and leave within any given amount of time.
2. Since no matter can be created or destroyed as one attempts to remove unwanted material from one's living space, the remaining material mutates so as to occupy 30 to 50 percent more than its original volume. Dust breeds!
3. The odds are 6 to 5 that if one has late classes, one's roommate will have the earliest possible classes.
4. One's roommate (who has early classes) has an alarm clock that is louder than Gabriel's trumpet.
5. When one has an early class, one's roommate will invariably enter the room late at night and suddenly become hyperactive, ill, violent, or all three.

Some of Murphy's Laws

1. If anything can go wrong, it will.
2. Nothing is ever as simple as it seems.
3. Everything takes longer than you expect.
4. If there is a possibility of several things going wrong, the one that will go wrong first will be the one that will do the most damage.
5. Left to themselves, all things go from bad to worse.
6. If you play with something long enough, you will surely break it.
7. If everything seems to be going well, you have obviously overlooked something.
8. It is impossible to make anything foolproof, because fools are so ingenious.
9. If a great deal of time has been expended seeking the answer to a problem with the only result being failure, the answer will be immediately obvious to the first unqualified person.

"What's all that racket you're making in the pantry, Gerry?"

"I'm fighting temptation, Mom."

Two men were riding on a motorcycle. The one on the back kept complaining about being cold. The driver stopped and told him to put his leather jacket on backward to break the wind. He changed his coat and they started out again.

The motorcycle hit a rough spot in the road and the man on the back fell off. When the driver noticed his friend had disappeared, he went back to find him.

A big crowd had gathered around the man at the side of the road. The driver pushed his way through the crowd.

"Is he hurt?" he asked.

"I don't know," a man scratched his head. "He didn't seem to be in much trouble, but we turned his head around like it belonged and he hasn't spoken a word since!"

The new recruit was on guard duty with specific orders to admit no car unless it bore a special tag. He stopped a tagless car carrying top brass.

"Drive right through, driver," brusquely ordered the officer.

The recruit leaned down and peered at the high-ranking officer. "I'm new at this, sir," he apologized. "Do I shoot you or the driver?"

Computers

To err is human, but to really foul things up requires a computer.

The main impact of the computer has been the provision of unlimited jobs for clerks.

The Law of the Computer
If you put tomfoolery into a computer, nothing comes out but tomfoolery. Yet this tomfoolery, having passed through a very expensive machine, is somehow ennobled, and no one dares to criticize it.

One man's red tape is another man's system.

Courage

Courage: Playing a municipal golf course on a weekend without an anesthetic.

"This bunion will have to be removed," the doctor stated *callously*.

The ship was sinking, and the captain called all hands together. "Who among you can pray?" he asked.

"I can," replied an ensign.

"Then pray, shipmate," ordered the captain. "The rest of you put on the life jackets. We're one short."

"I'm not staying in this scary house overnight," he said *hauntingly*.

Dating

They strolled down the lane
together,
The sky was studded with stars.
They reached the gate in silence,
And he lifted up the bars.
She neither smiled nor thanked him,
For indeed she knew not how.
For he was just a farmer boy,
And she—a Jersey cow.

"How do baby chickens dance?"
   "Chick to chick, naturally."

A diamond may not be as tight as a tourniquet, but it certainly stops the wearer's circulation.

"Where was your big brother going with that bag of oats?"
   "Taking his girl out to dinner. He says she eats like a horse."

At bedtime, Mother was telling her son about when she was a little girl. The boy listened excitedly as Mom told of having a Shetland pony and a cart, going to a country fair, and swimming in the stream near the farm.
   Finally he sighed, "Gee, Mama, I wish I had met you earlier."

A young man's shirt was soaking wet when he picked up his date. "Why is your shirt so wet?" she asked.

He replied, "Well, the label inside says 'wash and wear.'"

"You will have a happier life," a father warned his pretty daughter, "if you avoid trying to convert a *boyfriend* into a *buy* friend."

A girl met an old flame at a party, and she decided to be a little sarcastic.

"Sorry," she murmured when the hostess introduced him to her, "I didn't get your name."

"I know you didn't," replied the ex-boyfriend, "but you certainly tried hard enough."

Dieting

You know you need to go on a diet if to get your panty hose off, you have to go down to the service station and be put up on the grease rack.

A happy dieter has other problems.

"I've gained over fifty pounds," he explained *roundly*.

You need to go on a diet when you keep dreaming that somebody named Captain Ahab is chasing you with a harpoon.

Messages to Yourself
(Put these on your mirror)

- Instead of counting calories aloud, count calories allowed.
- There's nothing like three squares a day to make you look round.
- Go put on last year's bathing suit and see if you still want chocolate fudge cake.

You are in trouble with your weight when you put a couple of lettuce leaves over a pizza and call it a salad.

You know you need to go on a diet when you're wearing red, white, and blue and someone asks if you played the backdrop in the movie *Patton*.

You may need to go on a diet when your friends want to play hide and seek, and you can only play seek.

A four-year-old was showing the family's new bathroom scale to a five-year-old.

"What is it?" asked the five-year-old.

"I don't know, but when Mommy and Daddy stand on it, it makes them mad."

You have a weight problem when your boyfriend suggests that, in your case, it takes *one* to tango.

"Dieting religiously" simply means you don't eat in church.

The Twinkie Diet: You are permitted to eat as many Twinkies as you like as long as you do not remove the cellophane.

The Chinese Food Diet: Eat soup with chopsticks. If you still put on weight, use only one chopstick.

The Seafood Diet: If you see food, don't eat it.

The Ecology Diet: You can lose weight by not eating, just like you can also avoid air pollution by not breathing.

QUESTION: How do you know when you have a weight problem?

ANSWER: When you're standing on a street corner dressed in your red, white, and blue dress and a little old lady comes up, forces your lips open, and shoves a letter into your mouth.

You know it's time for a diet when:

- you dive into a swimming pool so your friends can go surfing.
- you have to apply your lipstick with a paint roller.
- Weight Watchers demands your resignation.
- the bus driver asks you to sit on the other side because he wants to make a turn.

Then there was the fellow with weak eyes who put a coin in a parking meter and exclaimed, "Oh, my goodness. I've lost a hundred pounds!"

Embarrassment

BOY TO DRAFT BOARD: "But you can't turn me down. I've proposed to three girls, sold my car, and told my boss what I think of him."

"I wish I had left my wife home," Lot stated *saltily*.

A baby was yelling loudly in the service. A lady got up to take him out. The preacher protested, "Lady, that baby's not bothering me!"

She shouted back, "Well, you're bothering him!"

Charles was having trouble getting up in the morning so his doctor prescribed some pills. Charles took them, slept well, and was awake before he heard the alarm. He took his time getting to the office, strolled in, and said to the boss: "I didn't have a bit of trouble getting up this morning."

"That's fine," replied the boss, "but where were you yesterday?"

"Oh no! I'm standing in quicksand," the woman shouted *defeatedly*.

J.B.: "Why does a girl say she's been shopping when she hasn't bought a thing?"

STACY: "For the same reason a boy says he's been fishing."

The new hired hand spoke right up to his employer, "Your farming methods are terribly old-fashioned. I doubt if you'll get ten pounds of apples from that tree."

"I doubt it, too," said the farmer. "It's a peach tree."

A father and his son were walking along together and they met another man.

The boy asked the man, "Mister, are you from Texas?"

The man bowed his head and walked away.

The father said, "Don't ever ask a man if he is from Texas."

The boy asked, "Dad, what's wrong with that?"

"Son," said the father, "if he is from Texas he would let you know, and if he isn't he doesn't want to be embarrassed."

"What are the three words most often used by students?"

"I don't know."

"That's correct."

Exams

"I'm afraid you've flunked the test," the professor said *degradingly*.

A teacher, annoyed with his clock-watching students, covered the clock with cardboard on which he wrote: "Time will pass. Will you?"

When working toward the solution of a problem, it always helps if you know the answer—provided, of course, you know there is a problem!

PROFESSOR *(finishing long algebra problem):* "And so we find X equals zero."
Sophomore: "All that work for nothing?"

Teenage Philosophy
   I have yet to see any problem, however complicated, that, when you looked at it in the right way, did not become still more complicated.

If you think education is expensive—try ignorance!

Did you hear about the schoolteacher who made her husband take her for a drive on a mountain road while she corrected papers?

She liked to grade on the curve.

"What's the formula for water, Chuck?" asked the chemistry professor.

"$H I J K L M N O$," spelled the freshman student.

"Whatever are you driving at?" asked the professor. "Who gave you that idea?"

"You, sir," said Chuck. "You said yesterday it was H to O."

A high school student asked his teacher if a person should be punished for something he hadn't done.

"No," said the teacher. "Of course not."

"Good," said the boy. "I haven't done my homework."

A married college student, harassed by family and professors, was taking an examination in a psychology course. For several moments he puzzled over the question, "Give an example of mixed emotions."

Then he nodded and wrote quickly, "Watching your mother-in-law drive your new Cadillac off a cliff."

TEACHER: "How is the abbreviation 'etc.' used?"

MARK: "To make people think we know more about something than we really do."

A student, not knowing an answer to one of the questions on an exam—and having quite a rough time with the entire exam—wrote: "Sometimes an idiot can ask more questions than a wise man can answer."

"Too bad you flunked the test," said a high school student. "How far were you from the right answer?"

"Two seats!"

Forgetfulness

They say an elephant never forgets, but what's he got to remember?

"I forgot to mail the check to the electric company," the man said *delightedly*.

Harry, who was eighty-three, shot a great game of golf; but his eyesight was going, and he couldn't see where he hit the ball. He was advised to take Sam with him. Sam could no longer hit the ball, but his eyes were perfect. Harry hit the ball and turned to Sam, "Did you see where the ball went?"

Sam said, "Exactly."

"Where is it?" asked Harry.

"I forget," Sam answered.

The hired girl was sent down to the stream to fetch a pail of water, but she just stood there gazing at the water, apparently lost in thought.

"What's she waiting for?" asked the farmer's wife.

"I dunno," replied the farmer. "Maybe she hasn't seen a pailful she likes yet."

HITCHHIKER: "How far do you drive to work?"

ABSENT-MINDED PROFESSOR: "Oh, about fifteen minutes."

HITCHHIKER: "Excuse me, sir, could you give me the time?"

ABSENT-MINDED PROFESSOR: "Oh sure *(checking his watch),* I have about three miles."

A mother proudly introduced her son to a charity-committee friend. "This is my son. Isn't he a bright little boy?"

The youngster, quite accustomed to being shown off in public, purred, "What was that clever thing I said yesterday, Mother?"

Girls

Some high school students were asked to write down their favorite hymn.

One girl submitted, "Ted Miller."

What did the short-order cook give his girlfriend when they became engaged?

A 14-carat onion ring.

"If I read my daughter's mind correctly," stated a pastor, "our world during the millennium will be inhabited only by herself, a few chosen girlfriends, and multitudes of young boys with driver's licenses and sports cars."

What is the difference between a running girl and a running dog?

One wears a skirt—the other pants.

Did you hear about the little girl who asked the gift-card salesman, "Got anything in blank report cards?"

A local minister was preparing his sermons for Sunday morning and evening when his phone rang. The guest speaker who was to preach the baccalaureate sermon for a girls' school had been in an accident. The local minister assured the Dean he could be there in an hour.

While he was dressing, the minister told his wife to pick up the notes on the right side of the desk and put them in his Bible. A friend drove him to the girls' school and they discussed the accident of the guest speaker. The minister did not open his Bible until he stood up to speak.

Then, to his horror, he realized he had given his wife the wrong directions. The words of his text danced before his eyes.

"Follow me, and I will make you fishers of men."

Two high school boys were chatting during football practice:

"Nikki sure is a smart girl," remarked one to the other. "She has brains enough for two."

"Then she's just the girl for you," said the other.

A farmer's daughter had graduated from high school. The father wanted her to attend college, but the mother was very fearful. After much discussion, the mother reluctantly consented for the daughter to go to college.

The daughter hadn't been away too long before the mother received a letter. She ran out into the field where her husband was at work, waving the letter and calling to him.

The father said, "What in the world has happened?"

The mother replied, "She is going to marry a foreigner."

"How do you know?" he queried.

The mother held up the letter and said, "Listen, I'll read it to you." She said, "I have fallen in love with Ping-Pong."

"What are her measurements?"

"We don't know yet because we haven't had her surveyed."

Grandparents

A young girl had bought Grandma a Bible for Christmas and wanted to write a suitable inscription on the flyleaf. She thought and thought until suddenly she remembered that her father had a book with an inscription in it—a book of which he was proud. She decided to copy it. When Grandma opened her gift on Christmas morning, she found neatly inscribed: "To Grandma, with the compliments of the Author."

A grandfather presented his seven-year-old granddaughter with a doll for her birthday.

"Mama, look at the lovely doll Gran'pa gave me!" she squealed. "He's the best gran'pa in the world. When I grow up I'm going to marry him!"

"I'm afraid you can't do that, honey," said her mother. "You'd be marrying my father."

"But, Mommy," said the child, "you married mine!"

"Have you any grandchildren?" the old fellow asked as he boarded the airplane.

"Yes," the passenger replied.

Then the fellow went to another passenger and said, "Have you any grandchildren?"

"Yes" was the answer.

So he went to another, "Have you any grandchildren?"

"No."

"Move over," said the old gentleman happily. "I want to tell you all about mine."

My grandmother made a fruitcake out of floor wax. When my grandfather ate it, he died, but he sure did have a fine finish!

A grandmother went to visit her son's family. She had never seen her six-year-old grandson and was extremely anxious to make friends with him.

"Hello, there," she said when he met her at the door. "I am your grandmother on your daddy's side."

The youngster eyed the woman thoughtfully and shook his head. "You won't be here long before you find out you're on the wrong side."

JOLIE: "Grandma, if I was invited out to dinner, should I eat pie with a fork?"

GRANDMA: "Yes, indeed."

JOLIE: "You haven't got a pie in the house that I could practice on, have you, Grandma?"

An English teacher was having daily trouble with an unruly pupil, so she stopped by his home to speak with his parents.

The boy came to the door. She asked for his mother or father.

"They were here," he said, "but now they's gone."

"Where," she demanded, "is your grammar?"

"She's taking a nap," he answered.

Grooming and Wardrobe

"I'm sorry the plastic surgery was a failure," the doctor said *defacingly*.

A couple returned home from the morning worship service, and the wife remarked to her husband, "There was a woman in the pew ahead of us who had the identical dress I wore."

"Does this mean you must buy a new dress?" asked the understanding spouse.

"Well," she commented, "it would be cheaper than moving!"

"Some day my face will be on Mount Rushmore too," the man declared *stonily*.

Jimmy, a style-conscious fellow, asked his brother, "What do you think would go well with my purple and green golf socks?"

Pat answered, "Hip boots."

"All right. I'll dress in a tuxedo, but I'm still going to wear my tennis shoes," the teenager said *sneakily*.

A handsome young clergyman felt it his duty to reprimand the girls' Sunday School class about the way they dressed themselves. "The more experience I have with lipstick," he said, "the more distasteful I find it."

PROFESSOR: "What is the most outstanding contribution that chemistry has given the world?"
JOHN: "Blondes."

"How many times do I have to tell you—no starch?" the customer asked *stiffly*.

Confucius say: "Man who crosses ocean once and back again and doesn't take bath for entire time is 'dirty double crosser.'"

There's a new kind of beauty contest. The winner of third prize gets a two-weeks all-expense paid trip to Texas. The winner of second prize gets a one-week all-expense paid trip to Texas. The winner of first prize doesn't have to go!

Housework

A housewife was busy with spring cleaning when she was interrupted by the doorbell. Opening the door, she saw a smiling young man.

"Good morning! I'm selling books and . . ."

"Not interested!" the housewife snapped and slammed the door.

In a few minutes the doorbell rang again, and she was confronted by a salesman selling pots and pans. "Not interested!" she shouted, and slammed the door.

Five minutes later, the doorbell rang again. Furious, she went to the door, threw it open, and shouted at the man standing there, "I suppose you work for some ridiculous, idiotic organization too!"

"That's for you to decide," the man replied, "I'm your new pastor, ma'am."

"Is ink so very expensive, Father?" asked Stacy.

"Why, no, what makes you think so?"

"Well, mother seems quite disturbed because I spilled some on the hall carpet."

"I'll fix that blown fuse with this penny," he said *glowingly*.

Trouble strikes in series of threes, but when working around the house the next job after a series of threes is not the fourth job—it's the start of a brand-new series of threes.

In any household, junk accumulates to fill the space available for its storage.

Insults

"Did you fill in that blank yet?"

"What blank?"

"The one between your ears."

On a bus one evening a woman was bothering the driver every few minutes, reminding him where she wanted to get off.

"How will I know when we get to my street?" she asked.

He couldn't resist replying, "By the big smile on my face, lady."

Preachers treasure certain comments made to them by those leaving the church after a service. One pastor was told at the door, "I did enjoy that sermon; it was like a cup of cold water to a drowning man!"

Wayne, a college debater, was telling Scott about the upcoming debate in which he would participate.

"It's going to be something," he commented. "It will be a real battle of wits."

"How brave you are," replied Scott, "to go into a battle half-prepared."

"Let's play a game," Joey suggested to a friend.

"What game?" Jamie inquired.

"Let's see who can make the ugliest face."

"No, sir," Jamie said, "I'm not going to play that with you."

"Why not?" Joey asked, puzzled.

"Look in the mirror and see what a head start you've got on me."

"What's your name?" asked the store manager of the young boy who was applying for a job.

"Ford," replied the lad.

"And your first name?"

"Henry."

"Henry Ford, eh?" queried the manager with a smile. "That's a pretty well-known name."

The boy looked pleased. "Yes, sir, it should be," he replied proudly. "I've been delivering groceries around town for two years now."

If it can be borrowed and it can be broken, you will borrow it and you will break it.

"No, I don't get the best marks in school, Daddy. Do you get the best salary at your office?"

Jobs

Tips for Teenage Workers
> *From the electric bell:* "Never knock."
> *From the knife:* "Be sharp and bright."
> *From the barrel:* "Keep your head."
> *From the hen:* "Go out and scratch."
> *From the ice:* "Always keep cool."
> *From the crow bar:* "Open up."
> *From the mat:* "Step on it."
> *From the lawn mower:* "Push."
> *From the hammer:* "Drive."
> *From the yeast:* "Work."
> *From the pick:* "Dig."

One young lady told her mom she was in love with a boy in her class and was going to marry him.

"That's nice," said her mother, going along with the gag. "Does he have a job?"

"Oh, yes," replied the girl, "He erases the blackboard in our class."

"I'll connect this doohickey to the thingamabob, and that'll stop the clanging in the whatchamacallit, and that'll cost you two hundred dollars," the workman said *mechanically.*

"I don't like this offer the company made to me," the union leader said *strikingly*.

"I play a fourteen-foot-tall clown in the circus," the performer said *stiltedly*.

A store manager prided himself in his business and in the way he made his employees work. One day he came into the storeroom and saw a boy leaning against a pile of boxes.

"Boy," he said sharply, "how much salary do you get?"

"Thirty-five dollars a week," the boy answered.

The manager took thirty-five dollars out of the cash register and handed it to the boy, "Take that and get out of here."

When the boy had gone, the manager turned to another man. "How long has that kid been working here?" he asked.

"He don't work here," the man answered. "He just came by to leave those boxes."

"There, I've given the baby her bottle," the babysitter stated *decryingly*.

An old blacksmith realized he was soon going to quit working so hard. He picked out a strong young man to become his apprentice. The old fellow, however, was crabby and exacting.

"Don't ask me a lot of questions," he told the boy. "Just do whatever I tell you to do."

One day the old blacksmith took an iron out of the forge and laid it on the anvil. "Get the hammer over there," he said. "When I nod my head, hit it real good and hard."

Now the town is looking for a new blacksmith.

Kissing

During days of the "Wild West" a "bad hombre" entered a railroad coach, flourishing a sixgun in each hand, and bellowed, "I'm gonna rob every man on this train, and I'm gonna kiss every woman."

A determined-looking rancher rose and said, "Pardner, you can rob us men, but durned if you're gonna kiss the ladies."

A pert little lady interrupted the rancher, "Now leave him alone; *he's* robbing this train."

AUGIE: "Am I the first girl you ever kissed?"
DANNY: "Now that you mention it, you do look familiar."

> *It's done beneath the mistletoe,*
> *It's done beneath the rose.*
> *But the proper place to kiss, you*
> *   know,*
> *Is just beneath the nose.*

A teenage boy went to his doctor with an unusal complaint. "The first time I kissed my girlfriend," he reported, "I felt very warm and perspired. The second time I kissed her I felt very cold and shivered."

Pondering over this odd ailment, the doctor called the girlfriend and discussed it with her.

"You call yourself a doctor and you can't figure that one out?" the girlfriend asked. "There's nothing strange about it. The first time he kissed me was last summer, and the next time he kissed me was this winter."

"They do say," Mike began shyly, "that kisses are the language of love."

"Well, speak up," urged Linda.

An eager teenage boy at a party where the lights were dim saw a shapely girl alone in the corner. He edged up behind her and kissed her.

"How dare you!" she screamed, slapping his face.

"I beg your pardon," said the teenager. "I thought you were my sister."

"You idiot," she replied, "I am your sister!"

John was leading a cow. In addition he was carrying a washtub on his back, a chicken under his arm, and a cane in his hand.

Kim, his girlfriend, hesitated as they came to the woods. "Now, I'm afraid to walk with you in there. You might try to kiss me."

"How could I?" he assured her. "Look at all I'm carrying."

"But you could stick that cane in the ground, tie the cow to it, and put the chicken under the wash tub."

A pretty girl forgot her fare,
But the bus driver was not
rough. . . .
She kissed him sweetly then and
there,
And he said, "Fare enough."

An old army general and a young private got on the train. The only vacant seats were in the back of the car, facing an elderly lady and her granddaughter. During the day they all became well acquainted.

Late in the afternoon the train passed through a long tunnel. In the darkness there was the sound of a smack and a slap. When the train came out into the light, all four faces were red.

The grandmother thought: *That little upstart of a private tried to kiss my granddaughter, and she slapped him.*

The granddaughter thought: *That old general tried to kiss grandmother, and she slapped him.*

The general thought: *That young private tried to kiss that girl, and she slapped at him and hit me.*

When they got off the train, the private said to himself: *I never had it so good in my life. I kissed the back of my hand, slapped the stuffin' out of the general, and got away with it.*

Language

RANDY, *college student, to younger brother:*
"Hey, David, do you want me to tell you a narrative?"

DAVID: "What's a narrative?"

RANDY: "A narrative is a tale."

That night when going to bed, Randy asked, "Shall I extinguish the light?"

DAVID: "What does extinguish mean?"

RANDY: "Extinguish means to put out."

A few days later, David asked Randy, as a dog walked into the house, "Randy, do you want me to take that dog by the narrative and extinguish him?"

What did the mama broom and the papa broom say to the baby broom?

"Go to sweep."

"You must not use such language," a pastor said to a profane little boy. "Does your father swear like you do?"

"Oh, no, sir."

"When he is gardening," continued the minister, "and he steps backward on a rake and the handle flies up and hits him on the back of the head, what would he say?"

"Oh, he would just say, 'You're back early, dear!'"

Some high school students got into an argument about whether it was correct to say, "The hen is sitting" or "The hen is setting." They decided to ask a farmer which was correct.

The farmer scratched his head a minute and then answered, "You know, kids, that doesn't concern me a bit. What I want to know is, when a hen cackles is she laying or lying?"

The story is told of a certain society matron in Washington, D.C. At a banquet, she was seated next to a gentleman from China. Thinking she had to speak "pidgin English" to him, she sought to carry on a conversation.

When the soup course was served and had been consumed, she asked the Chinese gentleman, "Likee soupee?"

The gentleman, with true Oriental dignity, nodded and smiled, but said nothing.

After the salad course, she asked, "Likee saladee?" The same response came from the Chinese gentleman.

After the meat course, she asked, "Likee meatee?" The same response.

After the dessert, she asked, "Likee dessertee?" The same response.

Presently, the master of ceremonies presented the speaker of the evening. To the utter dismay of the lady, the speaker was her Chinese conversationalist. For thirty minutes he stood and in perfect, flawless, unaccented English delivered a masterful address. When he sat down he turned to her, smiled, bowed, and asked, "Likee speechee?"

Manners

A cute elevator operator, exposed for the umpteenth time to the remark, "I suppose you have your ups and downs," snapped back, "It's not the ups and downs that bother me. It's the jerks!"

Associate with well-mannered persons, and your manners will improve.

Run with decent folk, and your own decent instincts will be strengthened.

Keep the company of bums, and you will become a bum.

Hang around with rich people, and you will end up picking up the check and dying broke.

"You should never try to force-feed a lion," the trainer said *offhandedly*.

STEWARDESS: "Would you like to get on the plane now?"

FIRST-TIME PASSENGER: "No thanks. I'd rather get in the plane."

Two cars met head-on on a narrow, one-way bridge. Screeching to a halt, one irate driver stuck his head out the window and shouted, "I don't back up for idiots!"

Calmly putting his car in reverse, the other motorist replied, "I do."

Did you hear about the two shepherds who formed a partnership?

In the springtime they shear and shear alike.

DAD: "Son, what did you learn in school today?"
SON: "I learned to say, 'Yes, sir,' 'No, sir,' 'Yes, ma'am,' and 'No, ma'am.'"
DAD: "You did?"
SON: "Yeah!"

MOTHER: "Another bite like that, and you'll have to leave the table."
HUNGRY BOY: "Another bite like that, and I'll be through."

Anytime you see a young man open the car door for his girlfriend, either the car is new or the girlfriend is.

A mother asked her son, "Why are you holding up that slice of bread?"

"I'd like to propose a toast!" said the boy.

The boy finished his breakfast and then rushed off to school without washing his face.

His teacher looked at him and said, "You didn't wash your face. What would you say if I came to school with egg and jam all over my face?"

"Nothing," replied the boy. "I'd be too polite."

Ministers

A pastor was talking with a poor woman who was a devoted member, present at all services. He expressed his thanks for seeing her so attentive to the services every Sunday.

"Yes," she said. "It is such a rest after a long, hard week's work to come to church, sit down on the soft cushions, and not think about anything."

A youth minister was at the circus, asking about the performers' faith. "I have faith in you to do your dangerous work," said he. "You must have faith in God."

The tightrope walker asked, from high up in the tent, "Do you have faith in me to walk this rope?"

"Yes," said the youth minister.

"Do you think I can push this wheelbarrow as I walk across the tent on this high rope?"

"Yes, even that. I believe in you."

"Then climb up here, sir, and ride across in the wheelbarrow!"

The rabbi and the priest welcomed a new minister to town by taking him fishing at a nearby lake.

They got in the boat and rowed out from shore about twenty-five yards.

"Wait a minute," said the rabbi, "I left my minnow bucket on shore."

The rabbi jumped out of the boat, walked out across the water, retrieved his minnow bucket, walked back across the water, and jumped into the boat. The new minister was astounded!

"I left my fishing rod on shore," complained the priest. Whereupon, he jumped out of the boat, walked across the water, retrieved his rod, strode back across the water and into the boat without getting a drop of water on him. By this time the new minister was literally beside himself.

Do these guys have some sort of God-given power that I have never heard about? reasoned the new minister.

Determined not to be outdone by the rabbi and the priest, the minister yelled, "Wait a minute—I just want to try what you guys have been doing." He stepped out of the boat and sank to the bottom of the lake. Splashing and struggling to the surface, he yelled, "Help me!"

As the rabbi and the priest pulled the minister into the boat, one said to the other, "Do you think we ought to tell him about the rocks we've been walking on?"

A pastor of a large city church always preached exactly twenty-one minutes—never over, never under. His church members marveled that he could do this so consistently. They bragged about his wonderful timing.

Then one Sunday he preached an hour and fifteen minutes. After church a deacon hurried to the pastor.

"What's the matter?" he asked. "You always preach twenty-one minutes exactly. Today you preached an hour and fifteen minutes. How did it happen?"

The pastor sighed. "Every Sunday when I get up to preach, I put a cough drop in my mouth. The cough drop melts in twenty-one minutes, and that's the way I time my sermon." He cleared his throat and looked embarrassed. "My teenage son slipped a button into my pocket this morning."

One morning the pastor was preaching about a series of Old Testament characters. After more than an hour he came to Ezekiel.

"Now here is Ezekiel," he declared dramatically, "Where shall I place him?"

A man near the front of the church stood up. "Give him my seat," he said, "I'm going home."

A young man was asked to preach right before the Sunday morning service began. It was a big camp meeting and hundreds of people were on the grounds, but the main preacher had not arrived.

Scared half to death, the young preacher went to the bishop's tent. "What shall I do, Bishop?" he implored. "They've asked me to preach, but I don't have any sermon."

"Trust the Lord, young man," said the bishop with great dignity. "Just trust the Lord." The bishop marched out of his tent.

The young man picked up the bishop's Bible and turned through it, hoping to find an inspiring verse. He found some type-written sermon notes that he liked very much. So taking the bishop's Bible and notes he went to the service.

The young preacher amazed everyone with his sermon. The people crowded around him after the service. Then suddenly the bishop pushed his way through the crowd.

"Young man," the bishop thundered. "You preached my sermon that I was going to preach tonight! Now what am I going to do?"

"Trust the Lord, Bishop," the young man replied with dignity. "Just trust the Lord."

Music

BOSS: "Ben, I wish you wouldn't sing at your work."

BEN: "I wasn't working, sir—I was just singing."

"Can you read music?" the choirmaster asked *notably*.

"I play music every Sunday for my church," she replied *organically*.

He was in his youth choir singing Christmas carols.

"Leon! Leon!" he sang.

The boy next to him nudged him and whispered, "Stupid! Turn your book over—it's 'Noel! Noel!'"

The director of music for the fashionable downtown church not only directed the choir, he also conducted the thirty-piece church orchestra, often combining the two groups for a magnificent service. One night for rehearsal, he had the orchestra and one hour later, the choir.

Some of the choir members, upon arriving, overheard the instrumentalists. When the music director entered the choir room, the first soprano gushed, "That last little thing the orchestra did was so charming. I loved its wild abandon, its ultra-modern theme. Was it your own composition?"

"No," said the music director drily. "That was the violin section retuning their instruments."

A newspaper mistakenly reported that the soloist's "insipid" singing caused the congregation to "burst into applesauce."

A popular country-western singer announced his retirement recently. Reason: his adenoids cleared up!

The organist for the wedding was late. They waited and waited but finally couldn't wait any longer. The minister stepped out into the audience and asked a woman to play the organ.

"What shall I play?" she asked, excited.

"Anything appropriate," he answered.

She went to the organ and played, "The Fight Is On."

Parents

A first grader came home from his first day at school and told his mother he was never going back.

"What's the use of school?" he said. "I can't read and I can't write, and the teacher won't let me talk."

BROTHER: "I think we have company downstairs."
SISTER: "How do you know?"
BROTHER: "I just heard Mom laugh at one of Dad's jokes."

A henpecked husband was advised by a psychiatrist to assert himself. "You don't have to let your wife bully you," he said. "Go home and show her you're the boss."

The husband decided to take the doctor's advice. He went home, slammed the door, shook his fist in his wife's face, and growled, "From now on you're taking orders from me. I want my supper right now, and when you get it on the table, go upstairs and lay out my clothes. Tonight I am going out with the boys. You are going to stay at home where you belong. Another thing, you know who is going to tie my bow tie?"

"I certainly do," screamed the wife, "the undertaker."

Two men were discussing the activities of their wives.

"Is your wife an active member of the sewing circle?" one of them asked.

"No," the other shook his head. "She just sits there and sews."

A six-year-old boy watched his father change from a business suit to his tuxedo. Suddenly, the boy began crying.

"What's the matter?" asked his father.

"Daddy, please don't wear that suit. It always gives you such a headache the next morning!"

A lady drove through a red light and a policeman stopped her.

"That light means stop," he said sternly, "You have to obey the law. Haven't you ever driven before?"

"Well, Officer," she answered sweetly, "This is the first time I have driven from the front seat."

A small boy was walking along, crying bitterly. "What's the trouble, son?" asked a kindly gentleman.

"My mother lost her psychology book," explained the lad between sobs, "and now she's using her own judgment."

A woman got on the bus with six children. Naturally, the bus was delayed while the smaller ones crawled on. The bus driver had been delayed several times before on his route, and his irritation had mounted each time.

"Lady, are all these your children or is this a picnic?"

"Mister," she said wearily, "these are all my children, and, believe me, it's no picnic."

Pranks

"Shall I boil the new missionary?" asked the cannibal cook.

"Boil him?" cried the chief. "Of course not. He's a friar."

PROF: "I believe you missed my class yesterday."

ELIANA: "Why, no, I didn't, not in the least."

Susie ran to her mother crying, "Look! Amy put this frog in my bed!"

"Amy!" called the mother. "Why did you do that?"

"Well," said Amy, "I couldn't find a snake."

A ten-year-old boy was going to sell soda pop at the park, and asked his father if he could borrow a wrench.

"You mean a bottle opener, don't you?" suggested his father.

"No," said the boy, "a wrench. First I've got to turn off the water at all the drinking fountains."

MOTHER: "Why are you home from school so early?"

SON: "I was the only one who could answer a question."

MOTHER: "Oh, really? What was the question?"

SON: "Who threw the eraser at the principal?"

"I did my good deed for today, Mom. I put a tack on the teacher's chair."

"You consider that a good deed?" asked his horrified mother.

"Sure. Everybody in the class dislikes him."

A teenage fellow went to his uncle's garage and asked, "Could you lend me a few gallons of gas?"

"What do you need gas for?" asked the uncle.

"The school is burning."

Chopper came running into the kitchen yelling, "Mama, there's the funniest man in front of our house."

His mother said, "Is that so. What is he doing?"

"Well," said the boy, "he's just sitting on the sidewalk and yelling at a banana peel I left there!"

Puns

A young minister once prayed, "Lord, fill my mouth with the right stuff and nudge me when I've said enough."

One day when I answered the door I saw a little man in a brown suit. He smiled and introduced himself.

"I'm Corn of Corn and Corn Real Estate," he explained as I invited him inside the house. "I'm from Corn, Oklahoma."

"Oh, yes," I said, "I've heard of that place. Do you know where the town got its name?"

"I sure do," he answered enthusiastically. "It was named after my grandfather Corn, the first settler. He had a son who went out west for a visit and met a young girl named Miss Cobb.

"They fell in love, and Mr. Corn married Miss Cobb. When the baby came, they named it Nubbin. They bought a crib for little Nubbin and lined it with silk and tassels. The people would stalk by and say, 'Aw, shucks.'"

What did Noah say when the animals started climbing into the ark?

"Now I herd everything!"

A Sunday School teacher was presenting the story of Lot. She related how God told Lot to take his wife and flee from the city. Unfortunately, she looked back and was turned into a pillar of salt. The teacher paused and Michelle asked, "What happened to the flea?"

A woman without a man is like a fish without a bicycle.

No books are lost by lending except those you particularly wanted to keep.

The two kinds of wood that make a match: He would and she would.

If at first you don't succeed, blame it on the teacher.

The good-humored minister in England said, "I can make a pun on any subject. Will someone name a subject?"

A man called out, "The Queen!"

The minister replied quickly, "The Queen is not a subject!"

It's always darkest just before the light goes out.

Then there was the man who for years kept changing his will. Seems he was a fresh heir fiend.

> There once was a lady named
>   Perkins,
> Who had a great fondness for
>   gherkins.
> She went out to tea
> And ate twenty-three,
> Which pickled her internal
>   workin's.

Whistler came in and found his mother scrubbing the floor. "Why, Mother," he remarked, "you're off your rocker!"

"Is Ballpoint really the name of your pig?"
"No, that's just his pen name."

A cannibal warrior felt depressed and went to his witch doctor. After listening to him for some time, the primitive medicine man observed, "The trouble with you is that you're just fed up with people."

If you throw a blue stone into the Red Sea, what will it become?
    Wet.

school

A school principal saw some boys huddled together. "What are you doing?" he demanded.

"We were telling dirty jokes," was the sheepish answer.

"Oh, that's all right. I thought you were praying."

SENIOR: "I passed Shakespeare today."
FRESHMAN: "Did he say hello?"

What do they call folks who never return borrowed books?

Bookkeepers

Kevin, while doing his homework, inquired, "Hey, Dad, what is the distance to the nearest star?"

"I really don't know," answered his father.

"Well, I hope you'll feel sorry tomorrow when I'm getting punished for your ignorance."

"Dad, can you write in the dark?"

"Of course, son. What do you want me to write?"

"Your name on my report card."

A college education won't hurt you if you're willing to learn something later.

It was the youngster's first day at school, and the experience proved too much for her. She returned home with her face down to the floor.

"What's the matter, honey?" her mother asked. "Didn't you like school?"

"No!" the first grader answered.

"Ah, I'll bet you were homesick," mother said.

"No," replied the child. "Schoolsick!"

Secrets

The Secrets of Frisbee Throwing:

1. A powerful force in the world is that of a disc straining to land under a car, just beyond reach.
2. The higher the quality of a catch or the comment it receives, the greater the probability of a crummy rethrow.
3. One must never precede any maneuver by a comment more predictable than, "Watch this!"
4. The higher the costs of hitting any object, the greater the certainty it will be struck.
5. The best catches are never seen.
6. The best single aid to distance is for the disc to be going in a direction you didn't want.
7. The most powerful hex words in the sport are: "I really have this down—watch."
8. In any crowd of spectators, at least one will suggest that razor blades could be attached to the disc.
9. The greater your need to make a good catch, the greater the probability your partner will deliver his worst throw.
10. The single most difficult move with a disc is to put it down.

"Dad, give me a dollar."

"Not today, Son, not today."

"Dad, if you give me a quarter, I'll tell you what the milkman said to Mama this morning."

"Here, Son, quick—what did he say?"

"He said, 'Lady, how much milk do you want this morning?'"

QUESTION: How do you catch a unique rabbit?

ANSWER: U-nique up on it.

People will believe anything if you whisper it.

Sisters

A small boy's definition of conscience: "Something that makes you tell your mother before your sister does."

A little girl had been praying every night for weeks, asking God to please send her a baby sister. One day she was taken to her mother's room to see her new twin sisters. The little girl was delighted. That night, she prayed like this: "Dear God, thank You for sending me a baby sister, but I thought You would like to know that she arrived in two pieces!"

Sleep

MINISTER: "I noticed your husband walked out in the middle of my sermon. I hope I didn't offend him."

WOMAN: "Don't worry about my husband. He's been sleepwalking since he was a child!"

"You other six dwarfs can stay up if you want to, but I'm going to bed," he announced *sleepily*.

Mother: "My son sleeps on the sofa all the time. One whole side of his body is covered with mohair burns."

Why did the little boy tiptoe past the medicine chest?

He was afraid he'd awaken the *sleeping* pills.

An eighteen-year-old soldier was given guard duty one night. He did his best for a while, but in the early morning he went to sleep. He awakened to find his superior standing over him.

Remembering the heavy penalty for being asleep on guard duty, this smart-thinking young man kept his head bowed for another moment, then looked piously upward and reverently intoned, "A-a-a-a-men!"

I came from a town so small they had to quit ringing the 9:00 P.M. curfew bell because it was waking everyone up.
Why was Dracula so sleepy?

He kept biting people who had tired blood.

A woman went to a psychiatrist and told him that her husband thought he was a refrigerator. "It isn't so bad," she said, "except that he leaves his door open and the light keeps me awake all night."

A sophomore, a junior, and a senior were driving across the country when their car broke down. They asked a nearby farmer if they could sleep in his spare bedroom. The farmer grudgingly agreed, but he said, "You all better be quiet, though. I don't like prowlers. I don't like noise. I'm liable to shoot first and ask questions later."

The three agreed not to make any noise and laid down to sleep. Eventually, the senior had to get up for a drink of water. As he stumbled down the stairs in the dark, he heard the farmer load his rifle and shout, "Who's that?"

"Meow," said the senior, and the farmer went back to bed.

A little while later the junior had to get up for a drink of water. The same thing happened. The farmer yelled, "Who's that?" The junior calmed him down by making like a cat, "Meow, meow."

Later in the night the sophomore had to get up too, and at the foot of the stairs he heard the farmer yell, "Who's that?"

The sophomore calmly replied, "It's me —the cat!"

Sports

Bill and Joe had been running buddies for twenty years. One day Joe wondered out loud if there was running in heaven. They made a vow that the first to die would somehow send a message back to the survivor. Two months later Bill passed away, and for weeks Joe was in mourning.

One night Joe was awakened by Bill's voice. "Tell me, Bill, is there running in heaven?" Joe wanted to know.

"I have good news and bad news," the ghostly Bill replied. "The good news is that there's plenty of running in heaven. The bad news is that you're anchoring our relay team, starting tomorrow."

The preacher said to a group of boys, "Remember always, that it is more blessed to give than to receive. Do you all agree with that?"

"I sure do," answered one boy. "My dad uses that motto in his business all the time."

The pastor beamed, "Ah, isn't that fine? And what is your father's business?"

Replied the boy, "He's a boxer."

After an hour of trying, the boy finally launched his kite. Then all of a sudden the wind died down.

"Oh please, God," he prayed, "no matter what You do, don't stop breathing now."

PETE: "My girlfriend said she would be true to the end."
SAM: "What's wrong with that?"
PETE: "I'm a fullback."

"Did you hear the joke about the rope?"
    "No."
    "Skip it."

Telephone

A father answered the telephone and told his son, "This is the third time your girlfriend has called this evening."

The son replied, "And you say I don't communicate well."

The pastor's phone rang on New Year's Eve. He recognized the voice of one of his members.

The member requested, "Send me over a bottle of wine tonight."

The pastor replied, "This is the pastor."

The member shouted, "Pastor, what are you doing in a liquor store?"

"Hello . . . hello . . . Is that you, Sam?"

"Yeah, this is Sam."

"It doesn't sound like Sam."

"This is Sam."

"Are you sure this is Sam?"

"Certainly, this is Sam."

"Well listen, Sam, this is Bill. Lend me fifty dollars."

"All right. I'll tell Sam when he comes in."

One afternoon a boy wanted to go to the movies. To find out what picture was playing, he dialed Information.

"What's the number for the theatre?" asked the boy.

The operator gave him the number and then suggested that perhaps the next time he could find the number in the directory.

"Yes ma'am, I know," explained the boy, "but I have to stand on the phone book to reach the telephone."

"When does the library open?" the voice on the phone asked.

"At 9:00 A.M.," came the reply. "And what's the idea of calling in the middle of the night?"

"Not until 9:00 A.M.?" answered the caller.

"No," yelled the now wide-awake librarian. "Why do you want in before 9:00 A.M.?"

"Who wants to get in? I want to get out!"

A supervisor in charge of complaints at the telephone company received a call from a new customer: "I have much more phone cord than I need, and it gets in my way. I wonder if you would mind pulling in some of it from your end? I'll tell you when to stop."

One minister called another one long distance on the telephone. It was a parson-to-parson call.

Video Games

BIOLOGY MAJOR: "What goes 999 klunk, 999 klunk, 999 klunk?"

FRIEND: "Search me. A new video game?"

BIOLOGY MAJOR: "No. A centipede with a wooden leg."

A man died and went to heaven. Peter met him at the gate.

"You are in heaven now," Peter stated. "Just tell me what you want to do and I'll arrange it."

The man had always drifted from one job to another. "I want a permanent job," he answered promptly. "I don't care what you give me to do as long as it's permanent."

So Peter gave him a toothpick and told him to move the Rocky Mountains into the Atlantic Ocean. A few million years later he came back. "I want a permanent job," he insisted.

Peter gave him a spoon and told him to dip up the Pacific Ocean and put it into the Atlantic. A few million years later he came back again. "I told you I want something permanent," he said.

"All right, I'll fix you up," Peter answered.

"Go down to earth and find a teenager playing video games. Take him out to get a Coke, and wait until he pays for it!"

Miscellaneous

A Sunday School teacher told her class, "We are here on earth to help others!"

Libby asked, "Well, what are the others here for?"

If a bakery explodes in your face, what might you see?

A Napoleon blown apart.

What did the near-sighted porcupine say when it backed into a cactus?

"Pardon me, honey."

What did the painter say to the wall?

"One more crack like that, and I'll plaster you."

ADAM: "What shall we name this one?"
EVE: "Let's call it a rhinoceros."
ADAM: "Why?"
EVE: "Well, because it looks more like a rhinoceros than anything we've named yet."

Three rabbits lived together. One was named Foot, the second one Foot Foot, and the third was called Foot Foot Foot.

One day Foot was feeling quite badly, so Foot Foot and Foot Foot Foot took Foot to a doctor. After examining Foot, the doctor spoke to Foot Foot and Foot Foot Foot.

"I'm afraid there isn't much I can do for your friend," he said. "He's very sick."

Sure enough, after only a week, Foot died, and Foot Foot and Foot Foot Foot were upset. Then one morning the following month Foot Foot said to Foot Foot Foot, "I feel terrible."

So Foot Foot Foot packed up Foot Foot and took him off to another doctor.

"We'll get a good doctor this time," Foot Foot Foot said to Foot Foot. "That last one certainly didn't help Foot."

The new doctor gave Foot Foot a thorough physical examination and reported to Foot Foot Foot that Foot Foot was very ill indeed. Foot Foot Foot became hysterical. "You've just got to save him doctor! We already have one Foot in the grave!"

SHE: "This is an ideal spot for a picnic."
HE: "It must be. Fifty million insects can't be wrong."

Jones and Smith met on the street. They hadn't seen or heard from each other in a long time.

"How are you getting along?" Smith asked.

"Not so good," Jones answered mournfully.

"What's the matter?"

"I got married since I saw you last."

"Why, that's good," Smith beamed.

"Not so good," Jones shook his head. "She's older than I am."

"That's bad," Smith agreed.

"Not all bad. She had a lot of money."

"Oh, that's good," said Smith.

Jones sighed, "She wouldn't give me any of it."

"That is bad."

"Not so bad, she built us a fine house to live in."

"That is good," Smith brightened.

"Not so good. The house burned down last night."

"That is bad," Smith shook his head sadly.

"Not so bad," Jones brightened at last. "She was in it."

HE: "If you'll give me your telephone number, I'll call you up sometime."

SHE: "It's in the book."

HE: "Fine! What's your name?"

SHE: "That's in the book too."

HE: "Going to have dinner anywhere tonight?"

SHE: (eagerly): "Why, no, not that I know of."

HE: "Mercy, you'll be awfully hungry by morning!"

POLICEMAN: "Miss, you were doing sixty miles an hour!"

SHE: "Oh, isn't that wonderful? I only learned to drive yesterday!"

DAD: "Son, did you have the car out last night?"

SON: "Yes, Dad, I drove some of the boys around."

DAD: "Really? Well, tell them I found two of their lipsticks."

GEORGE: "Man, I wish I could afford a car like this!"

JUD (the owner): "So do I!"

COUNTRY GIRL: "Mr. Jones, I'd like you to meet my boyfriend, Gene Gush, from the city."

VILLAGE POSTMASTER: "Shake my hand, boy. You sure do write a tremendous love letter!"

DAUGHTER: "What kind of husband would you advise me to get?"

MOTHER: "You get a single man, and let the husbands alone!"

MOTHER: "Yes, dear, I assure you that your father is the only man who has ever kissed me."

DAUGHTER: "Really, Mom, are you bragging or complaining?"

"There's a girl who suffers for her beliefs."

"Why, what kind of religion does she have?"

"I wouldn't quite call it religion. She just believes that she can wear a size 7 shoe on a size 9 foot!"

"What do girls talk about when they're together?"

"About the same thing boys talk about."

"That's terrible!"

DAUGHTER: "Jack makes me feel tired."
MOTHER: "It's your own fault, darling. You should stop chasing after him."

KIM: "What's your worst sin?"
DEBBIE: "My vanity, as the Bible calls it. I spend hours before the mirror admiring my beauty."
KIM: "That isn't vanity—that's imagination!"

Do you girls really like conceited men better than the other kind?"
"What other kind?"

SHE: "Dear, I'm so sorry I treated you the way I did. Please forgive me for being so angry with you all last week."
HE: "Hey, that's all right. I saved about forty-five dollars while we weren't seeing each other!"

SHE: "I certainly can't think about marrying you—or going steady with you, 'cause I don't love you. But I'll be a sister to you."
HE: "Wonderful. How much do you think our father is likely to leave us?"

SHE: "And are mine the only lips you've ever kissed?"

HE: "Yes, and they're the sweetest of all!"

HAL: "So she's going to marry that guy Harley. At least six girls have already broken up with the poor guy."

PETE: "Well, I guess it's just a case of being well shaken before taken."

JOE: "How come you go steady with Betty?"

ROB: "She's different from other girls."

JOE: "How's that?"

ROB: "She's the only girl who'll go with me!"

"Do you love me, darling?"

"With all of my heart, baby."

"Would you die for me?"

"No, sweetheart. Mine is an *undying* love."

"Give me a kiss, darling."

"No, no. My mother is against kissing."

"But, baby, I don't want to kiss your mother!"

FRANK: "I dreamed last night that I proposed marriage to you. What's that a sign of?"

DOT: "That's a sign that you've got more sense when you're asleep than when you're awake!"

John was in the middle of an English literature course. He and his girlfriend, Mona, were sitting on a bench facing the ocean. Becoming poetic, John came out with:

> *"Roll on, thou deep and dark blue ocean, Roll."*

About that time a huge wave began coming in, at which Mona squealed, "Oh, darling, it did. It did!"

ESKIMO BOYFRIEND: "What would you say if I told you I had come a hundred miles through ice and snow with my dog team, just to tell you I love you?"

ESKIMO GIRL: "I'd say that's a whole lot of mush!"

"How come you look so worried?"

"I'm trying to make up my mind about going to a wedding tomorrow."

"Who's getting married?"

"I am!"

BOYFRIEND (in late hours): "Baby, how can I ever leave you?"

TIRED MOTHER (poking her head around the door): "Bus No. 30 or Thumb No. 1 or 2!"

"Sweetheart, if I'd known that tunnel was so long, I'd have given you a kiss."

"My goodness, you mean that wasn't you?"

HE: "There are an awful lot of girls who don't want to go steady."

SHE: "How do you know?"

HE: "I've asked them."

JILL: "I'm going with an Irish boy."

JANE: "Oh, really?"

JILL: "No, O'Riley."

YOUNG WOMAN: "I've been asked to get married many times."

YOUNG MAN: "Who asked you?"

YOUNG WOMAN: "Mom and Dad."

BIG BROTHER: "Tommy, the parakeet has disappeared."

LITTLE BROTHER (TOMMY): "That's funny. It was there just now when I tried to clean it with the vacuum cleaner!"

LITTLE JOAN (to big sister Mary): "Sis, what do the angels in heaven do?"

MARY: "Why, they sing and play harps."

LITTLE JOAN: "Good grief, you mean they don't have TV or radio?"

JASON: "No kidding? You mean that trumpet actually earns you a weekly income? Do you play in a band?"

BOB: "I don't need to play in a band. Dad pays me several bucks a week *not* to play it!"

SUNDAY SCHOOL TEACHER: "Methuselah was 969 years old."

LITTLE CINDY: "What ever became of all his birthday and Christmas presents?"

BABYSITTER: "What're you kids doing?"

KIDS: "We're playing church."

BABYSITTER: "But you're not supposed to whisper in church."

KIDS: "Oh, it's OK; we're the choir!"

HAROLD (calling his dad at the office): "Hello, who's this?"

DAD (recognizing Harold's voice): "Why, it's the smartest man in the world!"

HAROLD: "Sorry, I can see I've got the wrong number."

BOY: "Why don't you come to our church?"

SECOND BOY: "Because we belong to another abomination."

LEANN: "Say, Mom, how much am I worth?"

MOM: "Oh, you're worth a million to me, honey!"

LEANN: "Oh, that's way too much. Just let me have ten dollars on next month's allowance."

MOTHER: "Will, I'm upset with you. I just heard you've been fighting with one of the boys next door, and you've given him a black eye."

WILL: "Yes, ma'am. You see, they're twins, and I wanted some way to tell 'em apart."

Little Bobby was sitting with his mother in church during the wedding of Bobby's oldest sister. Halfway through the service Bobby noticed his mother crying.

"Whatcha crying for, Mom? It ain't your wedding!"

FOND MOTHER: "Yes, Sally is taking French and algebra. Say 'Good morning' to Mrs. Smith in algebra, dear."

GRANDSON: "Grandpa, did you once have hair like snow?"
GRANDPA: "Yes, my boy."
GRANDSON: "Well, who shoveled it off?"

MINISTER: "Do you say your prayers every night, Egbert?"
EGBERT: "No sir. Some nights I can't think of anything I want."

MOTHER (to teenage son): "Mike, how many times must I tell you that you're supposed to keep your eyes closed during the prayer?"
MIKE: "Yeah, Mom, but how do you know I don't?"

A high school girl, seated next to an astronomer at a dinner, asked him, "What do you do for a living?"

"I study astronomy."

"My, my," she replied. "I finished that last year."

"Dad, what's your birthstone?"

"A grindstone, Son."

"What do you mean by coming in so late?" asked the irate father.

"Oh, Dad," he came back, "I forgot to tell you—I knew you wouldn't mind—I was sitting up with the sick son of the sick man you are always telling mother you sat up with!"

DAUGHTER (having received a mink collar from her father): "What I don't see is how such wonderful fur can come from such a low, sneaking little beast."

FATHER: "I don't ask for thanks, dear, but I do insist on a little respect."

FATHER (to loafing son): "You ought to be ashamed. When George Washington was your age, he had become a surveyor and was hard at work."

SON: "And when he was your age, he was president of the United States!"

MOTHER: "I had a heart-to-heart talk with our daughter about the facts of life."

FATHER: "Well, did you learn anything new?"

FATHER: "And why were you penalized at school?"

SON: "'Cause I didn't know where the Azores were."

FATHER: "From now on out, try to remember where you've put your things."

TEACHER: "Gretchen, tell me where the elephant is found."

GRETCHEN: "Good grief, Teacher, the elephant is such a large animal that he's very seldom lost!"

TEACHER: "Herman, what is a cannibal?"

HERMAN: "I don't know, ma'am."

TEACHER: "Well, if you ate your father and mother, what would you be?"

HERMAN: "An orphan, ma'am?"

TEACHER: "There will be only a half-day school this morning."

PUPILS: "Hooray! whoopee! Great! Tremendous!"

TEACHER: "Quiet! We'll have the other half this afternoon."

HILDA: "He's just bashful. Why don't you give him a little encouragement?"

BETSY: "Encouragement? He's so dead he needs an entire cheering section complete with a band and pom-pom girls."

GUY IN CAR: "Hello, sweet thing; want a ride?"

GIRL ON FOOT: "No way. I'm walking back from a ride now!"

ED (in court for speeding): "But, Judge, it's simply in me to do everything fast."

JUDGE: "If you don't slow down, we'll see how fast you can do thirty days."

SHE: "Did anyone ever tell you how wonderful you are?"

HE: "Don't believe they ever did."

SHE: "Then where'd you get that idea?"

He dropped by to a girl's house and was confronted by her little brother.

"Hi, Billy," he greeted the boy.

"Hi," the boy answered.

"Billy, is your sister expecting me?"

"Yep."

"How do you know?"

"She got outta here just a little while ago."

CARLOTTA: "What kind of car does your boyfriend, Tom, have?"

DOT: "A 'pray-as-you-go' one."

HE: "What's that book the conductor keeps looking at?"

SHE: "That's the score of the overture."

HE: "Who's winning?"

"Say it. Say you love me. Say it! Say it! Please say it!"

"It!"

JEANIE: "Aren't you getting Johnny and Bill confused?"

FRAN: "Yes, I get Johnny confused one night and Bill the next."

HE: "Could you learn to care for a guy like me?"
SHE: "If he wasn't too much like you."

GAL: "I wouldn't leave my happy home for any man."
GUY: "Then, after we marry, we could live right here with your folks!"

DAD: "What are your boyfriend's intentions, Daughter?"
DAUGHTER: "Well, he's been pretty much keeping me in the dark."

SHE: "Now that we're engaged, dear, you'll give me a ring, won't you?"
HE: "Sure, darling, by all means. What's your phone number?"

FIRST MAN: "She said I'm handsome, macho, and suave. She tells me that all the time."
SECOND MAN: "You shouldn't go with a woman who habitually lies."

HE: "There are two men I really admire."
SHE (with sarcasm): "And who's the other?"

HE: "You should see the altar of our church."
SHE: "Lead me to it."

HE: "I know I'm not much to look at."
SHE: "But after we marry, you'll be at work all day!"

HE *(having kissed her):* "Ah, that was indeed a triumph of mind over matter!"
SHE: "Yeah, I didn't mind, because you didn't matter."

HARRY: "She sure gave you dirty looks."
JERRY: "Who?"
HARRY: "Mother Nature."

SHE: "John, dear, I wouldn't let anyone else kiss me like this."
HE: "I beg your pardon. My name's not John."